Little Sure Shot

by Michael Burgan
illustrated by Robert Casilla

⇌ Chapters ⇌

◿Harcourt

Orlando   Boston   Dallas   Chicago   San Diego

Visit *The Learning Site!*
www.harcourtschool.com

Annie Oakley and the Wild West ⟞

In the 1880s people around the world knew of America's West. They had heard tales about ranchers and their cattle. They pictured horses filling a corral or a cowboy riding across the plains.

Not everyone had a chance to actually visit the West. Instead, western adventure came to them. Traveling shows brought talented riders and ropers to curious city viewers. In these Wild West shows, Native Americans, Mexican Americans, cowboys, and cowgirls performed for thousands of people.

One of the most interesting Wild West stars was Annie Oakley. Annie was a sharpshooter. She performed in Wild West shows and contests most of her life. Annie could hit a dime tossed into the air from 90 feet away. Annie was also an excellent rider who trained her horses to do tricks.

Despite her great skills, Annie never bragged about herself. To her, being polite and acting like a lady was as important as being a great performer.

Annie Oakley was born on August 13, 1860, in Darke County, Ohio. Her real name was Phoebe Ann Mosey. Her parents were farmers who struggled to feed their seven children. Consequently, the children helped out by tending to the farm animals and gathering nuts and berries.

Life became even harder for Annie in 1866. Her father died that year, and the family moved to a smaller farm. There was no money to buy food at the market.

Although she was not yet seven years old, Annie found a way to help her mother. She tied together thick cornstalks to make a small trap. Then she headed to the fields and caught animals for the family to eat.

One day Annie decided to take her father's old rifle and go hunting for food in the woods. Her mother didn't think she should use a gun and made Annie put the rifle away. Annie, though, was determined. If she didn't find food soon, her family would have nothing to eat. Within months she was back in the woods, looking for food.

When she was fifteen, Annie went to visit her older sister Lydia, who lived near Cincinnati, Ohio. Lydia and her husband encouraged Annie to enter a shooting contest. Until now, Annie had only used her gun for hunting. She had never shot at the clay disks called "pigeons" that were used in shooting matches. Still, she decided to enter the contest, which offered a prize of $50. In 1875 that was a lot of money. Today the prize would be worth more than $700.

Annie faced Frank Butler in the contest. He claimed to be one of the best sharpshooters in America. Frank was surprised to see his opponent was a young girl. He soon realized that this young girl knew how to hit a target.

Frank shot first. The pigeon was launched from a machine, and Frank hit it. Now it was Annie's turn. The pigeon soared and—bang! Annie had her first hit. The two shooters continued to take turns. Stray aim caused Frank to miss his last shot. Annie, however, finished with a perfect score.

Years later, Annie said she won more than a contest that day. She also won a husband. She and Frank began to date, fell in love, and were married in 1882.

Frank often performed in theaters, working with a partner named John Graham. One day, Graham became sick and could not perform, so Annie took his place on stage. She and Frank agreed that they would take turns hitting targets on stage. Annie's career as a performer had begun.

On stage, Annie decided to use a new name. She called herself "Annie Oakley" for the first time.

For their shows, Frank taught Annie new shooting tricks. The couple also used their pet poodle, George, in their act. Either Annie or Frank would shoot at an apple. When the apple broke into pieces, George would catch part of it with his mouth before it hit the ground.

Sitting Bull and Buffalo Bill

In 1884 Annie and Frank traveled to Minnesota, where they met the famous Sioux chief named Sitting Bull. In 1876 he had led the Sioux to victory against U.S. troops in the Battle of Little Big Horn.

Sitting Bull admired Annie's skill. He gave her the nickname "Little Sure Shot." Sitting Bull also adopted Annie as his daughter.

The next year Annie and Frank joined a Wild West show led by William Cody. Everyone knew Cody as Buffalo Bill.

Cody had been a soldier and a scout in the West. He was a sharpshooter, too. Because Cody could think like a businessman, he knew people would pay to see Wild West events on a stage. His show, called Buffalo Bill's Wild West, traveled across America.

Annie quickly became the star of the show. She helped Cody make a profit with his business. Most days Annie performed in front of thousands of people. In her act Frank tossed up targets for her.

Buffalo Bill's show also featured Native Americans. Sitting Bull was briefly a part of the show, and other Sioux performed. Cody created villages in the arena, so people could see how Native Americans lived. He also staged battles and paraded buffalo in front of the crowd.

In 1887 Cody took his show to England. Annie met Queen Victoria, who called Annie "a very clever little girl."

After the trip to England, Annie left Cody's show. However, she continued to perform on stage. Cody's show, though, was certainly the best, and Annie returned to it in 1889. The show grew bigger than ever, as the performers acted out bits of history from the West. Annie continued to do her shooting and riding tricks.

Annie and the cowgirls who performed helped attract women and children to the show. They showed Americans that women played an important role in the West.

Life After the Wild West Show ⇥

Over the years Annie won many contests. On her chest she proudly wore the medals she had received for her victories. Annie amazed people with her sure aim.

By 1901, however, Annie was ready to stop her public performances. Her decision to leave Buffalo Bill's show became easier after Annie injured her back in a train accident. The injury slowed her down, and after that she shot mostly in contests or special events.

In 1913 Annie and Frank stopped working together on stage for good. Annie was ready for a quiet life—or so she thought. At first, she and Frank tried to relax, but soon Annie was spending her time riding and hunting.

Annie also began teaching other women how to shoot. After the United States entered World War I in 1917, Annie offered to find women willing to fight.

In 1922 Annie once again performed on stage for a huge audience. She was still "Little Sure Shot."

A Look at Annie's Life

1860—Annie is born on August 13 in
　　　　Darke County, Ohio
1866—Her father dies
1875—Annie defeats Frank Butler in
　　　　a shooting contest

1882—Annie, now married to Frank,
　　　　joins his stage performance
1885—Annie and Frank join Buffalo Bill's
　　　　Wild West show
1887—Annie travels to England with
　　　　the Wild West show

1901—Annie leaves Buffalo Bill's
　　　　Wild West Show for good
1913—Annie and Frank stop working
　　　　together on stage
1926—Annie dies on November 3

Annie Oakley died on
November 3, 1926. Since then,
many writers have described Annie's
life. Not everything written about Annie is true. Some
people do not realize that Annie was not a real cowgirl.
Still, she will always be connected with the Old West.

Annie was a woman ahead of her time. She won
fame for doing things many people thought only men
could do.